BLUFF YOUR WAY
IN
PUBLIC SPEAKING

CHRIS STEWARD &
MIKE WILKINSON

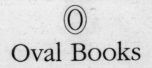

Oval Books

Published by Oval Books
335 Kennington Road
London SE11 4QE

Telephone: (0171) 582 7123
Fax: (0171) 582 1022
E-mail: ovalbooks.com

First published by Ravette Publishing.
This edition published by Oval Books.

First edition 1988
Reprinted 1991
Revised 1992
Reprinted 1993, 1995
Revised and updated 1997
Reprinted 1998
Second edition 1999

Series Editor – Anne Tauté

Cover design – Jim Wire, Quantum
Printing & binding – Cox & Wyman Ltd.

The Bluffer's Guides® series is based
on an original idea by Peter Wolfe.

The Bluffer's Guide®, The Bluffer's
Guides®, Bluffer's®, and Bluff Your
Way® are Registered Trademarks.

CONTENTS

The Speech   6
Preparing the Speech   8
Structuring the Speech   9
Memorising the Speech   17
The Case for Cards   21
Rehearsing the Speech   22

Types of Public Speaker   24
The Hyena   24
The Elephant   25
The Peacock   25
The Camel   26
The Squirrel   27
The Mouse   28
The Aardvark   30

Public Speaking Occasions   32
After Dinner   32
Company Presentations   33
Company Conferences   34
Public Symposiums   34
Weddings   35
Memorials   38

The Audience   39

Presentation   43
Overcoming Nerves   43
Delivery   44
Taking Questions   46

Deviation and Distraction   51

Planned Interruptions   51

Unplanned Interruptions   52

Tactics   54

Do's and Don'ts   56

Glossary   59

INTRODUCTION

In a recent survey public speaking came top of the list of worst things that can happen to you. It even ranked ahead of dying.

Although public speaking can arise in many forms, there is one factor ever present. Most would say that this is the need to communicate something to the audience, but it is immediately clear that these people have never been in an audience when a so-called expert (in reality, a probable bluffer) has been speaking.

The reality is to be found much nearer home. As any public speaker, or halfway decent bluffer will tell you, the ever present factor is one of sheer terror. No matter what the occasion or the subject matter, the poor wretch at the front is on his or her feet because no-one else is stupid enough to do it. So this book will:

1. Act as a warning beacon to the unwary who might be tempted to say 'Yes' to a public speaking invitation without realising what they have let themselves in for.

2. Act as a guide to the naïve or foolhardy who are thinking, 'I've accepted. Now what do I do?'

3. Convince you that things are never as bad as they seem.

4. Console those people who have no choice. i.e. bridegrooms, best men, corporate presenters, etc.

5. Help you become an expert bluffer in your own right.

It is intended to be useful whether you are giving your first speech, or your forty first. Whether you are talking to two, or two hundred. Whether you want to, or not.

THE SPEECH

Much has been written, and spoken, by the experts on the art of public speaking. Remember that these people take the whole thing far too seriously for their own good. Public speaking is there to be enjoyed, provided it is approached in the right manner. Success, and turning disaster into triumph, is virtually guaranteed if close attention is paid to the following recommendations.

Preparing the Speech

A veritable army of expert bluffers, masquerading as speech writers or script consultants have convinced most people that preparing and planning the speech is pretty difficult. This is why they are expert bluffers.

The first thing the one who wants to do well at public speaking must learn is that preparing speeches is, in fact, a fairly straightforward process involving two steps:

1. **Decide what subject matter to speak on**.

This may, of course, be predetermined by someone else. The subject may be one with which you are familiar, e.g. corporate management, or it may be one about which you know absolutely nothing, e.g. corporate management. Either way, it does not matter. Armed with a few simple tips you will confidently tackle the topic at hand in the full and certain knowledge that few people in the audience will be any the wiser.

2. **Decide what to say about the subject**.

This is easier if you happen to know something about it, but do not be daunted if you do not. Many professionals have made a handsome living out of speaking on subjects they know nothing about. Politicians and television personalities are fine examples of this.

For some this may appear an over simplistic approach to preparation. If this is the case, there now follows a detailed examination of the complex considerations you need to undertake in order to make you feel better.

The Method

Bluffers know that nothing acts as a spur quite so much as a sense of achievement – in this case, a pile of paper developing rapidly before you. So, having acquired a large, lined pad, start a fresh sheet of paper every time you think of a point you want to make. In this way:

a) the order of each point can be shuffled about until it is in a satisfactory sequence.

b) if you put down a totally irrelevant or useless thought (and there will be many), it can be cast out without destroying the rest of the speech.

c) it gives the impression to any casual onlooker, let alone yourself, that you are making a great deal of progress.

7

It is not important at this stage either, to have fully developed notes: simply your first thoughts on each point.

At a later date, or from time to time, you can re-read each page, and add to it. In due course, you will find that you have inadvertently accumulated a sufficient quantity to form the entire speech.

The Message

There are two common misconceptions concerning the message that you may have either read or heard. The first is that speeches and presentations should have one (a message, that is) and the second is that what you are saying should have some relevance to the audience.

Extensive audience research would tend to discount both. In a recent poll of the twenty three people at a party political rally, thirteen were asleep, four said it was warmer than under the railway arches, and the remaining six were a group of lost orienteerers from Wigan.

It is easy to be fooled into believing the people who propagate such arguments are right. The problem is that if you do believe them, you are going to have to undertake significantly greater amounts of preparation than is actually necessary.

Since it is widely accepted that the best solutions are usually the simplest, this is what you should be looking for. Remember that speeches and presentations with no message require the absolute minimum by way of preparation. The benefits of approaching presentations in this highly positive and open-minded fashion are numerous.

- Operating without the constraints of a message allows you to be much more creative in your thinking.

- You can never be accused of provoking dissent if you don't actually make any points.

- Once you have written one good speech with no message or relevance to anyone, you can use it over and over again thus saving even more valuable preparation time.

The sort of compliment the true bluffer should be seeking is encapsulated in these few words from Winston Churchill, the epitome of the public speaking bluffer.

> 'He can best be described as one of those orators who, before they get up, do not know what they are going to say; when they are speaking, do not know what they are saying; and, when they have sat down, do not know what they have said.'

This is the sort of compliment the sensible bluffer works towards. You now have a target at which to aim.

Structuring the Speech

Custom has it that speeches and presentations should have a beginning, a middle, and an end. This may sound obvious, but many public speakers do not appear to have a beginning, and even fewer have an end.

9

Many audiences are only aware that the speech is over when they are awakened by people clapping around them. At this point bluffers in the audience will turn to a neighbour and comment on how thought-provoking they found the speaker to be. If you are tempted to do this you should be aware of the risks. Your neighbour might have been awake.

Public speakers should concentrate their energy on getting the opening and closing phrases right because they know that these are the only two parts the audience hears. In between times, they can happily read extracts from last week's football results, and will not be put off by minor outbreaks of snoring.

They also know that they can capture audience interest at any time they like, by using the immortal words:

'...and so to summarise', or
'...and so in closing'.

Either phrase will command immediate attention and can be used any number of times in the same presentation.

The Start

Writing the start to a speech can often be tricky. Having scribbled out 'Good morning/evening, ladies and gentlemen', you can sit and stare at the blank sheet in front of you for ever.

Alternatively, you could pick up the daily newspaper. This will have been written and edited by comrades in bluff, known as journalists, and captures the essence of any subject in the opening line or two of every article, inviting you to continue reading to the end.

Amateur speakers can learn much about starting speeches from a few minutes browsing among the national press. Here is a random selection from several newspapers to give you the general idea:

'Five prisoners were preparing to spend their second night on the roof of Risley remand centre last night.'
The Daily Telegraph

'Millions of people are living beyond their means, and are hopelessly in debt says a recent report.'
Banking Weekly

'Soaring quantities of cocaine confirmed that Britain is becoming the drogs headquarters of Europe, added a smokespan.'
The Grauniad

'Even the police officers present were forced to flee as the orgy raged. One ran round the corner with his trousers round his ankles, while others hid their faces.'
The Sun

Starting an after dinner speech or business presentation with any of these lines would not be good form, but the erstwhile speaker should be trying to gain the attention of the audience by outlining the context or content of the talk in an interesting way.

Opening lines need only hold the audience for the first minute or two of the speech. This is because most audiences have the same concentration span as gerbils, and rapidly lose interest after this time.

The Finish

A major mistake is to end the presentation or speech with a weak 'thank you' and sit down. Successful speakers try to end on a note of drama, knowing as they do that the ending will be one of the rare moments when anyone in the audience is paying the slightest attention.

Ending on a positive note is always important, but particularly so if the purpose of the speech is to persuade the audience to a point of view or course of action. This could include:-

a) supporting a proposal
b) recommending action
c) appealing for money.

All speakers know that as the end of the speech approaches, the single use of a phrase like 'In summary then, ladies and gentlemen', will waken the audience from its torpor as effectively as a sniff of smelling salts.

Pausing for a moment to let them gather their thoughts, you can launch boldly into a reaffirmation of the one or two key points from the speech. Remembering that all audiences want to know what is in it for them, you end triumphantly on the dazzling array of benefits to be gained from adopting the recommended course of action or idea. Among the more popular benefits that attract audiences to support proposals, recommendations and appeals, are:-

1. The implied threat of having to go over it all again, in case they did not understand the first time.

2. An easier life. (This is always popular.)

3. Knowledge. Knowing something of which very few others are aware is a hallmark of geniuses and bluffers.

4. Money. There is a direct relationship between the amount of money being offered and the amount of support it will generate. In the more esoteric reaches of global quantum economics this is known as bribery.

5. The bar. There are two types of bar at the kind of events where bluffers are likely to be speaking, those that are free and those that are not. The former have a much greater pull than the latter.

Knowing this, most audiences can be persuaded to make difficult decisions by being reminding that the free bar closes in ten minutes. One word of warning, never use this technique when two conditions prevail:

a) You are addressing camels. (See types of public speaker.)

b) You are positioned between the audience and the bar.

Content

No matter what the content, most speeches are composed of an interpretation of something or other, and are often a personal view. A speech is not expected to be:

a) comprehensive, or
b) the last word on the subject.

This gives you an ideal opportunity for bluffing. One little-known pearl of obscure or irrelevant fact will have more impact and do your reputation more good than any amount of sensible information. Indeed, by delivering it, the speaker is presumed by listeners to know about the subject in depth.

Remember too, that as soon as you stand up to speak, the very act of doing so has 70 per cent of the audience believing that you are an authority on whatever it is you are supposed to speak about.

Form

Try to remember the KISS principle, i.e. Keep It Simple, Stupid. Think of any number of continually successful politicians: their speeches are often simple to the point of banality. If you subscribe to the view that your audience is likely to be simple this should work.

However, on the basis that experienced bluffers find it unnecessary to know a great deal about their subject, there is clearly a benefit in using as much jargon as possible. If this can be combined with a number of incomprehensible four or five syllable words, so much the better. The actual words used do not need to be connected to the subject in any way.

On the other hand when you come to the points in your speech that you understand, never use anything but the plain, everyday language you use with your friends. For the rest of the speech it is more effective, and infinitely more impressive, to substitute long words for short ones, such as:

participate	–	take part
finance	–	pay for
utilise	–	use
demonstrate	–	show
permit	–	let
relinquish	–	give up
manufacture	–	make
sufficient	–	enough
approximately	–	about
large-scale	–	big
moreover	–	what is more
nonetheless	–	but
however	–	but

unless, of course, you are clear about your subject and want your audience to comprehend it, in which case, do the opposite.

Quotes

Quoting someone famous, like Samuel Johnson or Jean-Paul Sartre, can be done, but is probably only for elementary bluffers since it is possible that someone in the audience knows more about the person being quoted or the context in which it was made, than you do.

It is much better to quote from someone less well known. In fact, the more obscure, the better. This not only makes it unlikely that anyone will ever have heard of your source, but allows you to misquote all over the place without anyone being any the wiser.

Repetition

Any gaps in the script can easily be covered by repeating something that has already been said, however many times. This may not only save a lot of writing, but may help reinforce a particularly hazy point you are making. It is also of benefit to the majority of the audience, who are certain to have been on mental autopilot the first time you said it.

A good ploy, often used by the really skilled speaker, is to make only one point, but to repeat it over, and over, and over again.

Anecdotes

An assortment of anecdotes can be used as fillers to pad out large chunks of the speech where you have nothing really interesting to say, or just have nothing to say at all.

They do not necessarily have to have anything to do with the subject at hand. As long as they can be linked to it in some way, this is enough.

If you want to hear this tactic demonstrated, simply follow the progress of an author on a promotional tour in any one week. You will hear the same favourite story repeated whether on radio or television, and if they can get away with it, so can you.

Memorising the Speech

The expert view seems bent on making life difficult for the public speaker. Not content with wanting you to spend hours in diligent preparation and research, and more time illustrating cue cards, they now suggest you memorise the important bits. This can only mean that they cannot read their own writing. What other possible reason can there be for memorising half your script?

The key here is to note that the only bits you are encouraged to memorise are the important bits. With no message and no relevance, there won't be any important bits for you to have to memorise and so once again you will have saved yourself valuable time by using the bluffer's guide.

The Case for Cards

This is not, as you might expect, a recommendation to give up all thought of making a speech and spend the time playing patience or strip pontoon, but a way of reminding yourself of what to say. It might be the last thing you want to know, but you will probably find it helpful if you have:

a) at least a brief recollection of the words you intend to use, and

b) a rough idea of the order in which you intend to use them.

The obvious thing to do in this situation is to write your speech out word by word and then read it.

If this is the case, why complicate things by using cue cards? Never underestimate the experts, because they have thought of an answer to this. Writing out speeches word by word, they say, is time consuming and results in a presentation that is thoroughly stupefying.

The astute will ask 'Isn't that the objective?' Of course it is, and examples of success in the field are all around us. For instance, politicians, and those other great stalwarts of the predictable speech, trades union officials, whose success rate in creating paralysing boredom is legendary. You would do well to emulate these speech-making gurus.

However, this is not the way for the expert. Enter the cue card. On each card you write a few words that act as a prompt, then make up the bits in the middle as you go along. The experts tell us that this makes your speech more natural.

Clearly, the longer your speech, the more cue cards you will need. The more cue cards, the greater the hazard. To add to the difficulty, many experts design a hieroglyphic code which they maintain is more effective than writing words.

But for bluffers who may be interested in this type of speech writing, and in order to present a balanced view of the options available, the following examples of key words and symbols may be helpful. You will notice that in most cases at least two interpretations are possible. The first is the meaning you intended when preparing the cue cards. The others are those that might cross your mind in the heat of the moment.

Symbol/ Key word	Interpretation
£	1) Talk about the financial implications. 2) Don't forget to ask the organiser for the money before going home.
!	1) Emphasise this point. 2) Get a new cricket bat.
∗	1) These are the main points. 2) Remember to watch tomorrow's episode of The Sky at Night.
†	1) These are the positive points in the argument. 2) If you add this lot together you end up with the square root of not a lot.
−	1) These are the negative points in the argument. 2) These are the negative arguments in the point.
?	1) Ask the audience a rhetorical question at this point. 2) What am I doing here? 3) What does this mean? 4) What time does the bar open?
⌗	1) Link this section of the script to the next. 2) Where is the fire escape?

Symbol/ Key word	Interpretation
V	1) Use a visual aid. 2) Oh my god, which one? 3) Time for a gesture. 4) Check audience hostility. (This symbol is often found on political cue cards.)
☺	1) Smile now. 2) Tell the one about . . . .
☹	1) Look earnest. 2) I should never have had the vindaloo.
S	1) Summarise at this point. 2) Stand for the applause. 3) Sit down. 4) Stay for the acclaim.
RUN	1) Run the audio visual sequence. 2) Wish it was possible.
• • •	1) Pause for effect. 2) Look at the next cue card.
INTRO	1) Introduce yourself and the subject of your speech. 2) Introduce, and hand over to, the next speaker. 3) Must get an introduction to the woman/man in the front row.

If you still believe that cue cards are the answer for you, one additional aid will be of interest. The experts having got themselves into this, rather than admit their mistake, decided to bluff their way out of it. The introduction of colour proved a masterstroke. None of their speeches proved any better, but numerous exhibitions of their by now surrealistic cue cards have been held at various Centres for the Performing Arts.

So now instead of simply having cue cards that appear totally confusing in one colour, you can confound yourself in several different shades. This, surprisingly, has a number of potential benefits:

1. Anyone looking at your cards could be mistaken for believing you were going to say something much more profound than will actually be the case.

2. The audience can be fooled into thinking that these cards were prepared by someone who knew what they were doing.

3. Having such accolades spoken aloud confers the quality stamp on the aspiring bluffer. Once you have mastered the art of preparing awe-inspiring cue cards you can nonchalantly leave them lying around in order to solicit further compliments.

The moral in this section is to do your own thing. If you want to bore the audience to death by writing and reading your own script word for word, then do it. On the other hand, if you want to dazzle them with your staggering wit and repartee, you would probably be best advised to steal someone else's.

Rehearsing the Speech

There is an old saying 'It'll be all right on the night'. Old hands know that this is because endless rehearsal and practice have made it good enough to be all right.

Practice will allow you to sound as if you know everything about the subject, especially if you do not. It will enable you to become totally confident in your delivery. Audiences are impressed by confident presenters.

Here are a few aids to successful performance.

1. Do it to yourself in front of a mirror.

This is not as peculiar as it sounds. A great many famous people have been doing it for years.

2. Use a tape recorder.

It's amazing how difficult talking to an inanimate plastic box can be. But take heart. At least it does not answer back. And if you think talking to a plastic box is difficult, just wait until you have an audience.

3. Video yourself.

If you think listening to a tape is hilarious, wait until you can hear and see yourself at the same time. Try to be self critical. Depending on whether it is an audio or video tape, there are one or two questions you should ask yourself:

a) Do I have any unpleasant habits I didn't know about? If you see yourself doing things you'd rather not see yourself doing, it's likely that an audience wouldn't want to see you doing them either.

b) How do I look?

It is said the camera never lies, but this is a time when you might wish it would bend the truth a little. There are people who have gone on instant fasts or spent the next ten months in a gymnasium after seeing themselves on video.

c) How do I sound?

Once you are over the shock that you don't sound like you, aim for sounding interesting. Practice introducing changes of pitch and pace into your speaking. Start singing in the bath. Join the local amateur operatic society. But whatever you do, do something.

4. Get yourself a prop.

Some people are fortunate enough to need glasses. If you are one of those who do not, get along to the opticians quickly. Glasses are a boon to the public speaker. Not only can you take them off, polish them and wave them about at critical moments, but they are also ideal as a 'dummy' substitute. There's nothing better than the odd suck on the ends to soothe the troubled brow and aid concentration. Well, almost nothing.

5. Force a friend or family to watch you rehearse.

This of course depends on the extent to which you are prepared to put relationships to the ultimate test. But the dedicated will never let such considerations stand in the way of recognition. Not to mention possible fees.

TYPES OF PUBLIC SPEAKER

Bluffers can gain enormous benefit from watching the antics of other public speakers before volunteering or being press-ganged into performing themselves. An exhaustive study has revealed the following public-speaking menagerie.

The Hyena

So called because of their irritating habit of laughing all the time, especially at their own stories. Hyenas get so engrossed in telling jokes and laughing at them, usually before the end, that they pay little or no attention to their audience. They cannot distinguish between one type of audience and another, so tell the same jokes to them all.

The monthly luncheon of the Clyst St Mary Ladies Sewing Circle gets the same treatment as the annual rugby club dinner. The hyena may begin with something slightly risqué, but soon progresses through sky blue to royal blue, and finally to purple.

There is something essentially pathetic about these people since they clearly believe that their capacity to tell jokes is somehow linked to their popularity as speakers. Their favourite phrase is; 'Have you heard the one about ...', and their most used phrase is; 'Now where was I?'

Hyenas almost always fail to notice that:

1. The audience is bored.
2. The audience is offended.
3. The audience has left.

Bluffers know that there is no connection between the capacity to tell jokes and popularity as a speaker. They also know that a witty line is usually more effective than a joke, and write down any they hear for future use.

The Elephant

Elephants are well known for their long memories. This type of speaker only knows a few subjects in any depth, but has long since committed these to memory. Unfortunately, the subjects they can speak on with any authority –

'How I helped relieve Mafeking'
'Famous Ethiopian stamps 1902 -1903'
'Laughs I have had with the Ayatollah Khomeini' –

no longer pack the crowds in.

As all speakers know, the speech must have some relevance to the audience, even if it is only marginal. The skill lies in making irrelevant information seem interesting. This is done by considering the audience composition, and tailoring the irrelevant directly to them.

The Peacock

No-one likes a smart-alec, and this is exactly what peacocks are. This is the 'look at me' brigade, whose unspoken motto is:

'Just give us the platform, and we will tell you everything you never wanted to know about the world, the universe, and anything.'

Peacocks love to strut about displaying their finery and their knowledge, and will accept the challenge of speaking on any subject under the sun at a moment's notice.

No self-respecting bluffers would ever want to be associated with peacocks. They will politely refuse any request to speak at short notice, even on the few subjects about which they know anything at all. Insisting on time to prepare properly to do the subject justice, they will get down to the local library to look up one or two interesting facts, or just get down to the local where a Peacock is bound to be holding sway. Here, for the price of a pint of lager, all sorts of attractive and extraneous facts may be proffered. You will only need one or two gems per speech, and you know where to put them for the greatest effect – at the beginning and at the end.

The Camel

As everyone knows, the camel can drink 20 gallons in ten minutes. What is less widely known is that there is a small but dedicated band of public speakers with a similar capacity. They only accept speaking invitations when:-

1. There is every prospect of an orgy of drinking of Bacchanalian proportions.

2. Overnight accommodation is provided afterwards.

It makes absolutely no difference at all to camels whether the speaking occasion is a wedding reception or the opening of a new branch of the Born Again Kamikaze Pilots Association, they are there to make absolutely certain the whole thing goes down with a pronounced slurp.

Bluffers hold differing views on the subject of drinking before, during or after speech making. The two broad approaches to this issue are:

a) To drink only water before and during the speech.

b) To get absolutely plastered before standing up to speak, on the basis that the drink acts as an anaesthetic, making it a relatively painless experience for the speaker. This may have the additional benefit of never being asked back.

The Squirrel

The reason these chirpy little rodents spend so much time digging small holes all over the place has nothing to do with burying food for the winter (a popular misconception easily refuted by any bluffer). It is that the stupid little creatures have completely forgotten where they left their nuts. Mind you, not being able to remember anything that happened more than two seconds ago, or being quite unable to grasp the concept of the future, must be a severe handicap.

A certain type of public speaker has developed a number of squirrel-like tendencies, allowing bluffers to gain a valuable insight from careful observation of them.

Among the lessons to be learned from watching squirrels are:

1. Have a spare copy of the script handy in case you forget yours. Get a friend or colleague to carry a copy if this is possible. Alternatively, send a copy to your host asking that it be kept close by 'just in case'. Your host should be impressed at your forethought and consideration, and might also take the hint and check the quality of the catering.

2. Do not try to cut corners, or be too clever. Write out exactly what you want to say. Shortening it on to cue cards may come later, assuming you have remembered to buy the cards.

3. Try memory training techniques. Mastering this can be immensely useful in recalling the words of long forgotten Mesopotamian poets, and using phrases like 'I'll never forget old whatsisname'.

4. Do not start looking for nuts during the speech, the results can be positively disastrous, not to mention highly embarrassing for everyone concerned.

The Mouse

This is the trembling, timorous speaker, who, peering nervously over the top of notes, squeaks at the audience.

Really expert speakers have perfected a few mouse-like habits, and use them on occasion to gain audience sympathy. Used sparingly, and with consummate skill, these may be helpful hints to those aspiring to true greatness:-

1. Develop a twitching nose. When combined with the twisting of a real or imaginary moustache, this technique can be absolutely devastating. It so distracts the audience that they fail to notice that the speaker is in fact reading from *Exchange and Mart*.

2. Wear very tight underpants to raise a normal voice to a squeak. The real problem arises when one has gained a degree of audience sympathy, and now wants to return to a normal speaking voice. Adjusting ones dress in front of an audience can be a very distressing business. In a famous case in Liverpool in the 1930s, a less than expert bluffer attempted three changes of voice pitch in one speech. At the subsequent trial, a plea of 'guilty' was entered and the defendant asked for 27 similar offences to be taken into consideration.

3. Practise changes of voice pitch in private. Ideally this should be done in front of a mirror to allow you to see what the audience is going to see. If anyone complains, or questions your sanity, remind them that consenting adults can do almost anything in the privacy of their own homes, and watch themselves doing it.

4. Compliment the host on the quality of the cheeseboard. This is not only polite, it allows you to demonstrate your knowledge (a little spread a very long way). Phrases such as 'blue veined', 'mould ripened', and 'nicely marbled' not only indicates expertise, but can be used on other occasions.

The Aardvark

This little African quadruped is noted for two things in particular, and so are the public speakers who have modelled themselves on the aardvark. The first is an armour plated skin, and the second is a tendency to grub around in ant hills.

Anyone who has faced a hostile audience will understand the value of armour plating, especially in deflecting awkward questions. It can also be very useful when you overrun on time, and the chairperson is trying to attract your attention. If the one point you want to make has not yet been covered, simply ignore the ever more frantic gestures from the chair, and carry on. If, as is more likely, there never was a point to make in the first place, you can acknowledge the chair and sit down.

Grubbing about in ant hills, or digging in the dirt, is one of the more useful attributes of public speakers. It is one of only two things that they have in common with the *Sun* newspaper, the other being the amount of titbits available. The real value of digging in the dirt lies in unearthing useful pieces of information that can be used to good effect. Here are some typical examples of the kind of thing bluffers will find helpful:

1. Is a fee being paid? If so, knowing in advance what it is will help in planning the strategy for getting it increased. If the fee being paid is small, it can be used as a sound reason either for not accepting the invitation or delivering the quality of speech the fee deserves. If no fee is being paid, suggest they book an acquaintance whose speech on 14th-century Serbo-Croat literature is said to be riveting.

2. Is accommodation provided? The answer to this question will be of special interest to camels, and to those with more than a passing interest in someone else's spouse.

3. How long is the speech expected to last? This will determine for example, whether it is possible to read from books, newspapers, magazines or telephone directories without anyone noticing.

4. What equipment is provided? This will help you in deciding the style of your speech or presentation. Always remember Murphy's Law: 'If anything can go wrong, it will'. The more equipment there is, the higher the chances of some minor disaster occurring. Clearly disasters that can be blamed on modern technology can be incorporated in your planning if you need an escape or excuse. Otherwise you would be well advised to check everything, at least twice, before you start to speak.

5. Who is the audience? It is very helpful to know this in advance since it allows you to dig into the subject and subsequently only say things which you know are not controversial. This has the added benefit of reducing the likelihood of there being any questions, since the audience can only agree with what you have said. Unfortunately it also tends to make for a staggeringly boring speech.

6. Information is power. This is never more so than when any information that is dug up can be used to the bluffer's advantage. In impolite circles this is referred to as blackmail. Bluffers prefer to call it tactical leverage.

PUBLIC SPEAKING OCCASIONS

There are basically two reasons why a bluffer may have to speak in public – for business or for pleasure.

Public speaking for pleasure is clearly a misnomer, since the only person in recent history known to have derived any pleasure from speaking in public committed suicide in a Berlin bunker in 1945.

Business

Business speaking occasions are those that either you are getting paid for or which you cannot avoid. They include:

After Dinner Speaking

Some people make huge amounts of money from doing this. Some people are very good at it, even if they do give the same speech over and over again. In this category, one would expect to find:

- retired sportsmen
- out of work actors
- television personalities
- failed captains of industry, and
- authors

who are professionals all, and being bluffers par excellence have no further need of help from us, if only because few, if any, of them are happy reading anything that they themselves have not written.

Those wanting to get into the after-dinner circuit should either:

a) have some sort of interesting job – like a mortuary attendant

b) have been featured in an exposé in *The Mirror* or *News of the World*.

If you fall into one of these two categories, offers of a free meal, expenses and a fee will soon come your way. Falling into both of them will guarantee bookings for at least the next year.

It is vital to remember that after-dinner audiences are the hardest of all to entertain. Preparation is all Never try to speak 'off the cuff': practise, practise and practise some more. If all else fails, insulting the guest of honour will always get a few appreciative cheers.

Company Presentations

These range from presenting new products to explaining next week's canteen menu. In its infinite wisdom, management assume that the best people to speak about these and sundry topics are those who know something about them. You are best advised to claim ignorance, or laryngitis, and volunteer a more junior member of staff. If a speech is totally unavoidable, remember this basic dictum:

'Tell 'em what you are going to tell 'em. Tell 'em. Then tell 'em what you have just told 'em.'

Company Conferences

The major difference between these and in-company presentations is that conferences are more discombobulating, grander, and far more expensive.

For these reasons, one should always try and speak at conferences. This is because:

a) every other speaker will be as bad, many far worse

b) no-one will be too interested in what you are saying and if you are a senior executive, the applause will be sycophantic and automatic

c) bluffers should only ever be associated with big budget events.

When you do speak at a conference, remember to keep it short so that the listeners can get on with the really serious business of enjoying themselves.

Public Symposiums

The definition of symposium is 'drinking party' which is precisely why most of the audience is there. Any notion that they have come to learn something is dispelled immediately by the numbers returning for the afternoon session.

You should take advantage of this knowledge by producing a glossy looking hand-out encapsulating a few choice words or phrases for use by audience members when asked afterwards by their superiors what it was the speaker actually said.

Social Speaking

Weddings

For most people weddings are the most likely venue for first forays into the world of public speaking. Fortunately, in most instances, they will also be the last. For those who volunteered their services, for whatever reason, or found there was little choice (concomitant with being on either end of a loaded shotgun) here follow some invaluable guidelines.

For the Groom

A bluffer in this role can make use of certain basic public sympathy as the entire wedding party, including the new bride, will be well aware that the groom is:

- still feeling the effects of his stag party

- terrified that he will not perform well in public, i.e. his speech

- terrified that he will not perform well in private, i.e. those quaintly named 'nuptials' – even if consummation has taken place some months, even years beforehand.

Essentially, the speech should cover five main topics:

1. **Romance**
How the bride and groom first met and fell in love. Never mind if it was not all that romantic make it up. Certainly the bride will not deny it.

2. **Diplomacy**
How the bride's family are so good, so kind, such obvious candidates for a Nobel Peace Prize. Lie.

3. **Sympathy**
How penniless the bride and groom will be in the future, having spent their hard-earned savings entirely on a new home, etc. but how they both know it was the Right Thing to do. (This part of the speech is aimed at rich Uncle Charlie.)

4. **Sex**
How wonderful. Stick to subtle innuendos, e.g. 'This will the the first night I've missed *News at Ten*.' Try to ignore the cynical smile on the face of the bride.

5. **Gratitude**
How generous. Thank everyone and anyone who is involved – for the presents, for being there, for remaining upright. Never make the mistake of thanking individuals by name for their presents, or even mentioning specific presents, because someone is bound to be left out, and this could start a family feud, yea even unto the fifth generation.

For the Best Man

The bluffer as best man is expected to be the real wit at the wedding. Do not be daunted. There are five rules that, if followed rigorously, can salvage the situation.

1. Deliver the speech while you are still relatively sober. Certainly never be more inebriated than your audience.

2. Keep it short. Only one or two amusing anecdotes in a slightly vicious, abridged, life-story of the groom. Never, ever be funny about the bride.

3. Do not tell jokes unless you are good at it, and unless you have practised them beforehand.

4. Use the telegrams. Most of these can be safely made up, since they are sent by people who either could not make it to the wedding, or were not asked. Both bride and groom will assume that they were sent by each other's friends and relations.

5. Vow not to be Best Man again. With this at the back of your mind, you will be able to approach your speech with something like relief.

For the Bride's Father

The bluffer in this role should not dwell upon one of life's great ironies – that not only is the bride's father expected to pay for everything, but he is also expected to make a spectacle of himself during the reception. Comfort yourself with the thought that, in this classic role, you have simply to cover three things – all of them short, sweet, and to the point:

1. How delighted you are to have so-and-so as a son-in-law. Even if you hated him on sight, and everyone knows it.

2 How much you (and your wife if she is (a) alive and (b) present) will miss your darling daughter. Try to look sincere, even if you feel like turning cartwheels.

3. How wonderful an institution marriage is. Even if you are awaiting your third divorce.

Then thank absolutely everyone for everything. Try to keep a list. If you find yourself at a loss, move smartly to the major toast of the day – not the caterers, but The Happy Couple.

Memorials

Funerals and memorial services are not easy for anyone asked to speak in public. The rule is to talk about the deceased in glowing terms, especially if you barely knew them. If you were genuinely close, find something private to share, and always relate a heart-warming anecdote (even if it has been embroidered a little – i.e. it happened to somebody else).

If the occasion is for someone who specifically asked that everyone should have a good time and you have to speak, leave the comedic approach to those who do it for a living. A little seriousness will do no harm, and will help comfort those who really are grief stricken. Aside from anything else, no bluffer should ever try to upstage a professional.

THE AUDIENCE

Bluffers should avoid the mesmeric approach to speaking as practised by Kapila Kumarasinghe, the well known raconteur and bon viveur, who held his audience spellbound for 150 hours while talking about Buddhist culture; or the open ended style, as evidenced by Paul Osgood, who, at a dinner in Liverpool, took 16 hours 6 minutes to respond to the toast to the guests.

It is therefore suggested that when making any speech or presentation, you consider your audience.

What is it the audience wants?

Most audiences want nothing more than to get away. Most speakers however, fail to recognise this basic requirement and proceed to speak for what can seem like weeks, on their given subject. You must be able to judge the mood of your audience, and have a handy escape route or sentence planned in advance.

The experienced public speaker will take advantage of the mood of the audience in one of two ways:

1. If the chairlady of the local Women's Institute meeting wants to know why your talk on computerised flower arranging only lasted three minutes, you can tell her that you sensed the audience had grasped the essential elements of your message, and now wanted a quick cup of tea and a biscuit before rushing home to put their new found skills into practice.

2. If you want to get your own back on someone, or guarantee that you will never be asked again, pick a subject that is broadly of no interest to anyone and make it last for as long as humanly possible. Whatever the mood of the audience when you started, by the time you have finished four and a half hours later they will know more about the natterjack toad than anyone else alive – except you.

Ideally, you should not include any slides or overheads since these might induce some flickering interest leading to a question for which you are quite unprepared. Worse still, the bright light might waken the audience before you are finished.

Subjects worthy of consideration could include:

'The Development of the English Concentric Castle'
'Hang-gliding in Holland'
'101 Things to do with a Butter Mountain'.

Why is the audience there?

There are numerous reasons why an audience might turn up to listen to you, or someone else, speak. Here is a selection of the most likely ones:

Coercion

Forcing part, or all of an audience to come and listen has been a feature of public speaking since lists of names were read out in that famous game featuring Romans, Christians and lions. Nine out of ten Christians who ventured an opinion said that they would rather be at Bognor. Since then, various others have thought up school assemblies, Communist Party Conferences, war crimes trials, and Barry Manilow concerts.

VIPs

These have always attracted large numbers, since there are people who seem to believe that being seen with someone important makes them important too. Bluffers should take heart from this because public speaking is one way to become really important and gather your own retinue of hangers-on who will be only too pleased to buy the drinks – just to be seen with you.

Sex

This has always been one of the great motivators. Business executives have been known to travel great distances to attend a wide variety of seminars, conferences and debates provided that two conditions prevail:

a) it means staying at an hotel.
b) members of the opposite sex are readily available.

Businessmen and their secretaries stand out like a red hat at a funeral at such events. They are so alert and attentive, at least to one another. Another give-away is when they ask for a copy of the script. This is a sure sign that they did not even bother to attend, but would like a copy of what was said in case they need an alibi.

Family Feasts

These events attract long forgotten relatives out of the woodwork like a plague of locusts. Every reception to celebrate the hatching, matching or dispatching of another member of the family becomes a re-creation of the Mongol hordes sweeping down from the steppes.

The key to success is to get the right speech for the occasion. Beginning with 'Dear friends, we are gathered here today to mourn the passing of ...' is hardly the way to get a fortieth birthday party dinner off to a rousing start.

Sales Conferences

The main reason this audience is here is because they are being paid. Company managers may congratulate themselves on staging an event the Royal Shakespeare Company would have been proud of, but they are fooling no-one but themselves. The audience wants to know several things, and will not hear anything else, however well it is packaged and presented. The questions they are framing in their minds are:

a) What time does the conference end?
b) Who is the after dinner cabaret?
c) What is next year's sales incentive?
e) Where on earth did they get these chairs?

Understanding your audience is a vital skill for the successful bluffer. In this respect bluffing bears a similarity with real public speaking.

PRESENTATION

Overcoming Nerves

The prospect of making a public speech or presentation can reduce normally sane and well-adjusted human beings to nervous wrecks. There are a number of things that can be done to eliminate this problem.

1. Do not turn up. This in itself is not enough. The true bluffer will combine this with a creative and original excuse that cannot be challenged, e.g. "I have been called away at short notice on a matter of state security." If you have any problems just mention the Official Secrets Act.

2. Have a stiff drink. Many people find that the combination of adrenalin and alcohol can have a dramatic effect on their performance. Not only does it reduce their nerves, it also seems to remove any inhibitions about what they should or should not say.

3. Breathe deeply. Care is required here in case your deep breathing is taken to indicate you are involved in some activity other than public speaking. A couple of deep breaths before you start can work wonders. Try it.

4. Exercise. Many public speaking experts will tell you that the best way to relax immediately prior to speaking is to deliberately tense the muscles in one

part of your body before relaxing them and moving on to another part. Do not be fooled by this: experienced speakers know that this is the quickest way to get cramp, and it is difficult to deliver a speech whilst writhing around in agony.

5. Shut your eyes. The experts will advise you to relax by closing your eyes and thinking of something serene and peaceful. This is all very well, but the observant will have spotted a similarity between this and going to sleep.

Delivery

This is the moment all good bluffers have been waiting for. The chairperson has just announced your name. You will now dazzle the audience with your apparent knowledge of the subject, pausing only once to sip the designer water, before retiring to thunderous applause and shouts of 'More, more'.

1. Walk smartly to the lectern or speaking position. The really experienced speaker will manage a small stumble to gain audience sympathy. This is because he knows he is going to need it.

2. Gather your thoughts. Standing at the lectern you should make sure that your notes are in order and ready to use. Do not rush this step. Time only makes your audience more excited at the prospect of hearing your words of wisdom. It also means you don't have to speak for quite as long.

3. Take two or three deep breaths. As already explained, the idea of this is to relax you prior to your presentation. In fact it makes the audience believe they are about to be addressed by someone imitating a goldfish. So whatever you say, they are going to be pleasantly surprised.

4. Make contact with the audience. If steps 1 to 3 have taken as long as they should have done, this contact may well need to be in the form of a seance. Otherwise it is most easily gained through eye contact. This means looking at the audience. The drawback here is that you are likely to realise that they are looking at you. If this makes you nervous, go back to Step 3.

5. Start speaking. Ideally this should be from your script, cue cards or an autocue. If you find that what you are saying is not linked with what was planned, do not be deterred. Clearly nerves have taken over so return to Step 3 and read the first paragraph or two whilst taking a few deep breaths. The accomplished speaker will do this in such a way that the audience believes he has paused for dramatic effect.

6. Speak slowly. This is an excellent technique for elongating speeches. The other, even more useful, benefit is that when you do eventually come to the point you can slow down even more, emphasising in two or three sentences what at normal speed would have taken up an entire page.

7. Look lively. Looking alive is a tenet central to the secret of successful public speaking. A few simple facial movements, like smiling or raising your eyebrows can also divert attention from the fact that your notes have got out of order and that you have just read page 3 before page 2.

8. Use pauses. Not necessarily in places that make any sense, but simply to break up the flow of words and to peer at your notes.

9. Keep going. Ideally the speaker should move from one unrelated point to another as smoothly as possible. This prevents members of the audience from focusing on the inconsistencies in the presentation, and from concentrating for too long on any one point, thus making it impossible for them to formulate any cogent questions.

Taking Questions

The first rule of sensible public speaking is don't. If you cannot get out of it, the second rule is don't take questions.

If you have followed our instructions carefully there should not be the remotest prospect of anyone asking a question since they will all be so muddled they shouldn't know where to start. In the unlikely event of anyone having understood any of what you said, any number of potential questioners may be put off for one or more of the following reasons. As a confident speaker you should do everything possible to encourage this state of affairs.

1. No-one wishes to appear foolish in front of everyone else by asking a question to which the answer might seem obvious to everyone except the questioner. Fear undoubtedly puts off a large number of questions. It can be spread rapidly throughout the audience provided you treat the first questioner as if he or she is some sort of mental defective. The only people this does not put off are mental defectives.

2. There is no time to deal with questions. Provided you have studied and put into practice the recommendations in this guide, this will be nothing more than the truth. If for some inexplicable reason you finish within the allotted time, you have only yourself to blame. But don't panic. If your reconnaissance of the venue has been effective you will know the location of the exits and the facilities. Now is the time to avail yourself of one or the other.

3. The speaker covered the points so well that everyone clearly understood. In the bluffer's case, this is an unlikely occurrence. It is more likely that you covered the points so well that everyone is thoroughly bewildered. Bewilderment almost always puts off questions since the questioner is usually under the misapprehension that he is the only one who is completely mystified. In this case, (1) above applies.

Bluffers are not silly enough to let the few people in the audience who were paying attention expose their scant knowledge of the subject matter by asking questions which they cannot answer. There are a number of ways to deal with this:

47

a) Right at the beginning of the presentation, say that there is so much matter to cover in the short time available that questions are impossible.

b) Explain that you will deal with questions at the end, having already arranged with a colleague to call you away just before you reach this point.

c) State that you are not as expert on this subject as you know some members of the audience to be. Of course, the risk here is that a number of people will wonder why you are speaking and not one of these experts. In all honesty you are probably wondering the same thing yourself. However, name them if possible. This not only allows them a moment of glory which earns you their unbounded gratitude, but it also allows you to call upon them to answer any awkward questions at the end.

d) Keep talking. If you are talking, the audience will not be able to ask questions. So if you fear there may be questions in the offing, keep talking. Clearly, the longer you make your speech the less likely questions become. There is no record of any questions being asked in Kapila Kumarasinghes' 159 hour Buddhist culture presentation. Obviously an expert at handling audience questions at his best.

If, despite having slavishly followed all the earlier recommendations, the audience is still sufficiently interested to ask questions you will only have yourself to blame. You will also have a question of your own. "How do I get myself out of this?" There are a number of techniques which you should find helpful:

1. The Politician's dance.

Thank the questioner profusely for asking such a significant question and then proceed to talk about something that is totally unrelated. This usually wins the day. If the questioner comes back suggesting you haven't really answered his question, simply do the same thing again. Given time, the questioner will give up.

2. What is the question? That is the question.

This comprises listening to the original question, and then telling the questioner what the question should really have been. This does not necessarily mean that either question needs to be answered but if you have to, you should make sure that you yourself can answer the question that you've just asked.

3. Don't listen.

This is perhaps the easiest of all the techniques, because it allows you to answer what you want to answer without the embarrassment of knowing that your answer has nothing to do with the question. As with (1) above, it is a particular skill of people in public life.

4. Never repeat the question.

Some people suggest that you repeat the question back to the questioner so that he understands that you understand the question. This is a bit like standing on the scaffold and helping the hangman make sure he has got the noose correctly round your neck. Don't do it. If the questioner knows that you understand the question, you will be at a significant disadvantage when asked why you haven't answered it.

5. **Make it long**.

If you do have to field a question, make your answer as long as possible. Quote large chunks of your speech all over again. With luck this will horrify the questioner and discourage anyone else.

DEVIATION AND DISTRACTION

Interruptions can completely throw the nervous speaker, but to the bluffer they are manna from heaven. Interruptions may be in one of two main forms – those that are contrived, and those that are not.

Planned Interruptions

Planned interruptions can be used to abbreviate the speech, or to end it completely. For example, suppose you were expected to speak for 15 minutes on the mating habits of the Antarctic Emperor Penguin, a common enough topic. After some research, a bit of note writing, and a rehearsal in front of the mirror, you discover that your speech only lasts 6 minutes. Using some of the techniques learned from reading this book, you can bluff this out to 10 minutes, but cannot think of another word. Do you:

a) Talk about something else for 5 minutes.

b) Invite the audience to meditate on what you've said for a few minutes.

c) Pause more often and for longer periods.

d) Show a visual aid of the subject matter in action.

e) End early.

If you really cannot think how to bluff your way through another 5 minutes, then you will have little option but to stage an interruption. For example:

1. For the consideration of some folding money, most catering staff will begin a round of the world plate-throwing championships next door.

2. Ask some friend or ally to send you a message that your office/home/car is on fire.

3. Plant a heckler in the audience.

4. Arrange for a stripogram.

5. Organise a power cut.

Ruses of this kind usually achieve two things simultaneously:-

– They prevent you from being able to finish.

– They gain you a good deal of audience sympathy.

Unplanned Interruptions

However thorough the research and planning has been, and however well rehearsed and prepared you are generally, there are numerous pitfalls awaiting the unwary public speaker. These range from minor noises off, which can be turned to your advantage, to colossal disturbances of the sort that might measure on the Richter scale.

When they do occur, you have several options. You can:

a) Go absolutely rigid with panic and forget everything before or after the event.

b) Give your impersonation of a goldfish.

c) Feign an attack of salmonella. If you are lucky enough to be getting paid, this ploy has the added benefit of obtaining a meal and a fee without doing any work.

d) Expertly bluff your way out of it.

The wise speaker will plan for all eventualities and have a witty line or two that can be used for any occasion. Here are a few situations that commonly arise, and some helpful ideas:

Telephone:
a) "If that's my stockbroker, tell him to sell."
b) "I told my wife/husband never to ring me at work."

Sirens/bells/fire alarms:
a) "So that's what happened to my early morning call."
b) "Is this what they meant by a hot audience?"

Aeroplanes/trains:
a) "I hope that's not the SAS arriving.

Breaking crockery or glass:
a) "I'm told all the waiters come from Greece."
b) "My wife/husband only ever throws one at a time."

Music:
a) "If a baton is available, I can conduct as well."

Dropped cards or notes:
a) "I never could play catch, either."
b) "We will now take a short break for a commercial."

Losing your place:
a) "My secretary complains about my writing, but I can't read her typing."
b) "You think you're confused? I don't know where I am either."

Tripping or falling on the way to the rostrum:
a) "President Ford used to do that for a living."

Projecting a slide upside down:
a) "That's what you get when you use an Australian photographer."

The microphone stops working:
a) "If the gentleman at the back could try listening a little harder ..."

Power cut:
a) "I seem to have overstayed my welcome."
b) "I know you're on a tight budget, but couldn't someone have fed the meter."
c) "Now we are *all* in the dark."

Tactics

Any number of tactics can be employed during the actual speech or presentation. The choice of which tactics to use will depend on the objective, the occasion, and how desperate you are. You need not go to any great trouble: the simplest solutions are often the most effective. Here is a random selection to choose from:

1. **Appearance**
Wear something outrageous such as an electric tie, (male) or jewellery designed to catch the light (female); or Dame Edna Everage glasses (either).

2. **Microphone**
The microphone is a potential match winner. Used creatively a tremendous range of whistles and ear-shattering screeches can be generated. Best of all, by holding the microphone an eighth of an inch from your lips, your entire speech can be rendered totally unintelligible.

3. **Mannerisms**
Distracting mannerisms are a god-send. If anything is going to take the audience's mind off the subject in hand it is a speaker who takes time to tweak his earlobes or scratch somewhere. This is simply because the audience becomes so engrossed in the presenter's peculiar peccadillos that the content becomes irrelevant. This assumes, of course, that it was ever relevant in the first place.

3. **Visual aids**
Here is a great opportunity to demonstrate a depth of knowledge that you don't possess. The real key to using visual aids is to make them as complicated as possible. This may countermand all you have previously heard or been taught, but the truly successful are always prepared to fly in the face of tradition.

Another established wisdom is that visual aids should illuminate the points being made by the speaker. But the experienced speaker realises that every audience contains at least one know-all who is desperate to display his or her own knowledge of the subject in depth, and linking the spoken word with visual images only encourages people like this to ask questions. You need to avoid this at all costs. As for illumination, the bluffer will ensure that there is as little as possible. Keeping the audience in the dark fits perfectly with the bluffer's strategy.

What visual aids mean in practice is that you can cover up your inability to speak coherently on one subject for more than three minutes, by employing a battery of special effects. With careful planning, these can last so long that there's no time left for your speech. You should view this as a positive point in your favour, because the audience most certainly will.

You need not rely on the interminable slides or acetates. Use a little imagination. If you have to talk about cricket to Americans, for example. Do you show slides of the last Test Match? Do you show them a cricket ball? No, you hold up a cricketer's box, and explain how and why it is used. Aside from the audience's appreciation of how dangerous a sport cricket is, the box will, suitably decorated, come in useful the next time you give a talk on medieval codpieces.

Do's and Don'ts

Do:

- Think up a good reason if you're late: being called away at the last minute for urgent talks at No.10 – never anything so mundane as a slow train.

- Go to the right place. This is a basic rule of success, not only for bluffers but for all speakers.

- Only ever make one point at a time. Audiences are incapable of grasping any more. Anyway, you're the one who is supposed to be doing the work.

Don't:

- Forget to thank your host, specially if you're being paid to speak, and you haven't received your fee yet.

- Spill any liquid into the microphone. At best, it will sound like the worst case of indigestion known to man. At worst, you'll electrocute yourself, thus cheating the audience of its entertainment.

- Tell jokes. Unless you are very, very good at them. (In other words, a level of competence greater than you would usually show, or expect from, friends at pubs or parties.)

- Use overworked clichés. Nothing in the world is truly original, but to say the same things as everyone else is tiresome, particularly for professional audience-goers who have to suffer this kind of thing several times each week just to get a few free meals. 'Unaccustomed as I am to public speaking', will only cause them to wonder why you are speaking in the first place.

- Use offensive language. What is acceptable on stag nights, or obligatory at rugby club dinners, will fall not on deaf but outraged ears anywhere else.

- Make personal attacks on, or even mildly derogatory remarks about any members of the audience.

Specially if they are bigger than you.

- Forget that every audience needs to be told why they should be listening to your speech. The fact that the doors have been locked is not considered sufficient reason. So tell them why they will enjoy or find interest in your speech; then give your speech; then tell them that they have enjoyed it or found it interesting. Who knows, if you sound convincing enough, they may actually believe you.

End Note

Having uttered the final sentence, do not flop meekly into your chair and wipe the perspiration from your brow. Milk the moment for all it is worth, and wait for the applause. When you judge this to be waning, smile, mouth a polite "thank you" and sit down in triumph.

From this experience it is possible to make four deductions concerning your ability to speak successfully in public, all of which are likely to be correct:

- You were much better than you thought you were going to be.

- Rather than the hostility or apathy you were expecting, the audience was warm and friendly, wanting you to do well. (This is because they have been thanking God that it was you up there and not them.)

- You actually enjoyed it.

- Bluffing works.

GLOSSARY

One of the delights of public speaking is that the part-time bluffer can become involved without having to learn vast amounts of jargon. This is a slight drawback to the full-time professional who may be disappointed at this apparent oversight. For both groups there follows a brief resumé of some of the words and phrases in regular use.

Audio-visual – Term that can be used in virtually any situation with the same degree of irrelevance. Provided something can be seen and heard, it doesn't really matter what, that's audio-visual.

Autocue – A device which allows your script to be projected on to what looks like a bullet-proof screen. A number of presenters have often wished it was.

Back projection – Flashy way of showing slides so that the audience can't see the projector. You have to put the slides in back to front so that they come out the right way round. If you put them in back to front in the same way you would if you were projecting from the front, they'd come out back to front.

Cue cards – A way of prompting yourself as to what it is you intend to say, but not necessarily the order in which you intend to say it. This depends upon the simple technique of numbering your cards or fixing them together with a treasury tag.

Delivery – Nothing to do with childbirth, although the sensations are probably remarkably similar. As every bluffer knows, content is nothing, delivery is all.

Lectern – The prop for your script. Some lecterns have been adapted for autocue. In this case you can't put your script on it, since it falls down the hole in the middle.

Overhead projector – Refer to OHPs if you want to be taken seriously. Most were designed by people with an intense dislike of the human race. They have a special feature which results in the bulb blowing after your third acetate. This is all good tactical stuff for two reasons: a) you'll never be asked to use it again, and b) the standard you have set will encourage others to make fools of themselves in the belief that they can't possibly do as badly as you did. Bet on it.

Acetate – The sheets of clear plastic which curl up at the edges the second you place them on the OHP. Also known as overheads, just to baffle the uninitiated.

Screen – The necessary object for projection. Trying to assemble a portable screen can only be accomplished with confidence by those who constructed the Forth Bridge. Those who have seen five grown men struggling with this equipment will know the truth of this. Never get involved in the practical aspects of projection screen erection. Taking a supervisory role, however, is to be encouraged.

Script – The poor man's autocue. Most schoolchildren could make the Kama Sutra sound boring. Most presenters can do the same with scripts.

Set – Much the same as a stage, but with the added complication of bits of hardboard, polystyrene and electric cables. The objective is to provide a suitable backdrop to the presentation. This is not always immediately evident. It provides a good living for set-builders, and a host of potential disaster areas for you.

Dissolve units – a) two Alka Seltzers in a glass of water; b) yet more expensive aids to allow slides to fade on and off the screen.

Structure – Not the building in which the fateful act is to take place, but the way in which your presentation is built up. It is said that speeches and presentations should have a beginning, middle and an end. If anyone insists, point out that if Ronald Reagan could do without it, then so can you.

Venue – The place where you are to perform, i.e. anywhere from a five star hotel Antigua, to the Balls Pond Road Assembly Rooms. Experienced bluffers will only accept invitations to speak at venues which enhance their reputation for bluffing, e.g. the Houses of Parliament or television studios; which involve payment; or which mean they can lie on the beach at someone else's expense.

Visual aids – The visual material you may use to brighten up an otherwise uninspiring speech or presentation. True bluffers will realise that there need be no correlation between their visual aids and what they are saying.

THE AUTHORS

Chris Steward was born in Dunstable, but after a petition by local residents, was forced to flee the country with his parents and finally rediscovered himself in New Zealand, Australia and Venezuela.

Having tried graphic arts, he stumbled into a sales and marketing career, attracted by the prospect of a company car and flexible expense account. With twenty years of blue-chip company experience behind him, and scaling new heights in originality, he set up the Steward Consulting Group. He now specialises in sales and marketing development and communication skills.

Mike Wilkinson was born in Bradford narrowly missing the Stanley Matthews Cup Final for which he has blamed his parents ever since. Having worked in the catering industry and local government, he was called to the bar at the Dairy Crest Annual Conference, where he found in his co-author a kindred spirit and enough money for the next round.

THE BLUFFER'S GUIDES®

Available at £2.99:

Accountancy

Personal Finance

The Classics

Philosophy

Computers

Public Speaking

Consultancy

The Quantum Universe

Cricket

The Rock Business

Doctoring

Rugby

Economics

Science

The EU

Seduction

The Flight Deck

Sex

Golf

Skiing

The Internet

Small Business

Jazz

Stocks & Shares

Law

Tax

Management

Teaching

Marketing

University

Men

Whisky

Music

Wine

Opera

Women